How to benefit from this book insha' Allah:

- This book is to help you learn about your creator. It is important to mention that Allah's names are not only the ones mentioned here but these are the authentic ones we know of.

- Each name is written in Arabic and English. In addition, the general meaning of the name is given. Where applicable some verses from the Qur'an that reflect the name have been included.

- It is encouraged that after you read about the name, to take time to reflect on it and how it is manifested in your life. There is space in the book for you to write your thoughts down.

- Each name has its own design to reflect how unique each name is and make it more appealing especially for the younger ages.

Disclaimer:

- Any good in this book is from Allah alone and not myself. And any bad or mistakes in this book are from myself and the devil. I ask Allah to accept this humble work and make it beneficial for us in this life and the next.

Allah

Allah

Keys to remember:

★ Allah, the name of all names. If you want to call on Allah with all his names, all his characteristics, all his majesty and greatness both what you know and what you don't then call on Him with his name, Allah. Such a beautiful word that you don't even need to move your lips to say, it's like it comes straight from the heart, straight from the soul.

★ Every type of worship we do has one main purpose and that is the remembrance of Allah. Our whole life revolves around the remembrance of Allah and trying to please Him. One of the best things you can do is remember Allah always as indicated in the following hadith,

Abu Darda (may Allah be pleased with him) narrated that the prophet (peace be upon him) said, "Should I not tell you of such a thing which would be among the best and purest deeds in the court of your Lord, high in ranks (darajat), better for you then spending gold and silver (in Allah's path), and better than slaying the neck of the enemy during war? The Sahaba said, "Yes, Oh Rasool Allah! ." He said, "It is Zikr of Allah." (Tirmizi)

How this name effects my life:

_____

_____

_____

Ar - Rahmaan

Ar-Rahmaan

The Compassionate, The Beneficent, The One who has plenty of mercy for the believers and the blasphemers in this world and especially for the believers in the hereafter.

Narrated by Abu Huraira:
I heard Allah's Apostle saying, Allah divided Mercy into one-hundred parts and He kept its ninety-nine parts with Him and sent down its one part on the earth, and because of that, its one single part, His creations are Merciful to each other, so that even the mare lifts up its hoofs away from its baby animal, lest it should trample on it."

Sahih Al-Bukhari (The Book of Good Manners) No. 5613

Keys to remember:

★ Allah is more merciful to us than anyone in the world even our parents.

★ Allah's mercy is for all creation whether they are Muslim or non Muslim or even animals.

★ One of the best ways to gain Allah's mercy is to show mercy to each other.

How this name effects my life:

___
___
___
___
___
___
___

Ar - Raheem

Ar-Raheem

The Most Merciful, The One who has plenty of mercy for the believers.

"And your god is one God. There is no deity [worthy of worship] except Him, the Entirely Merciful, the Especially Merciful."
(The Holy Quran 2,163)

"Say, [O Muhammad], "If you should love Allah, then follow me, [so] Allah will love you and forgive you your sins. And Allah is Forgiving and Merciful.""
(The Holy Quran 3,31)

Keys to remember:

★ Allah is specially merciful towards the believers so thank Allah always for this blessing.

★ At times of trial and hardship it may be difficult to remember how merciful Allah is, you may wonder why Allah has put you through all these trials. However, it is with Allah's mercy that we go through these trials. It is a constant reminder that this life is temporary and the real reward and real happiness is in the next life.

How this name effects my life:

_____
_____
_____
_____
_____
_____
_____

Al - Malik

الملك

Al-Malik

The King, the Monarch. The One with complete Dominion, The One Whose Dominion is clear from imperfection.

"So exalted is Allah , the Sovereign, the Truth; there is no deity except Him, Lord of the Noble Throne."

(The Holy Quran 23:116)

"Whatever is in the heavens and whatever is on the earth is exalting Allah , the Sovereign, the Pure, the Exalted in Might, the Wise."

(The Holy Quran 62:1)

Keys to remember:

- ★ Everything belongs to Allah, all of our belongings actually belong to Him. In reality we never truly own anything. That is why giving charity is just a way of giving back what rightfully belongs to Allah.

- ★ We should not fear anyone more than Allah as Allah is above everyone. And no one can do anything in His kingdom except by His will.

How this name effects my life:

_____
_____
_____
_____
_____
_____
_____

Al - Quddus

القدوس

Al-Quddus,

The Holy one. The One who is pure from any imperfection and clear from having children and adversaries.

"Whatever is in the heavens and whatever is on the earth is exalting Allah, the Sovereign, the Pure, the Exalted in Might, the Wise."

(The Holy Quran 62,1)

Allah is exalted above any resemblance to His creation in any way. This for certain includes having children and the like. Allah does not resemble anything we can imagine because anything we can think of will always be part of His creation.

Keys to remember:

★ Allah's beauty and reality is beyond our imagination and beyond anything in this world. But with Allah's mercy He has left signs all around us that are witness to His magnificence.

★ Seek to implement this name in your life by leading a pure life and dignifying Allah in everything you do.

How this name effects my life:

_____
_____
_____
_____
_____
_____
_____

Al - Salam

السلام

Al-Salam

The Peace, The Tranquility. The One who is free from every imperfection.

Allah is the perfect peace. He promises peace to the believers in this life and the next.

"Such people will be repaid for their steadfastness with the Highest Paradise, where they will be met with welcome and with Peace."
(The Holy Quran 25:75)

Keys to remember:

- Being truly happy is not with the amount of physical things we posses whether it be money, education, nice homes...etc. True happiness comes when the heart finds inner peace. This peace only comes with truly connecting with Allah and submitting to Him.

- Implementing this name in your life is being at peace with everything that Allah has written for you and everything around you.

How this name effects my life:

_____
_____
_____
_____
_____
_____
_____

Al - Mu'min

Al-Mu'min

The Faithful, The Trusted. The inspirer of faith. The One who witnessed for Himself that no one is God but Him. And He witnessed for His believers that they are truthful in their belief that no one is God but Him.

"God is He save whom there is no deity: the Sovereign Supreme, the Holy, the One with whom all salvation rests, the Giver of Faith, the One who determines what is true and false, the Almighty, the One who subdues wrong and restores right, the One to whom all greatness belongs! Utterly remote is God, in His limitless glory, from anything to which men may ascribe a share in His divinity!"

(The Holy Quran 59,23)

Keys to remember:

* Our prophet (pbuh) advised us to renew our faith with "la illaha illa Allah", there is no God but Allah. This is the corner stone of our faith that everything is built on and without it everything will come tumbling down.

* We will all sin as this is human nature. But what keeps us different from the non believers is our belief in the oneness of Allah, so never let go of that.

How this name effects my life:

_____
_____
_____
_____
_____
_____
_____

Al - Muhaymin

Al-Muhaymin

The Protector, The Vigilant, The Controller, The One who witnesses the sayings and deeds of His creatures.

"He is Allah, other than whom there is no deity, the Sovereign, the Pure, the Perfection, the Bestower of Faith, the Protector, the Exalted in Might, the Compeller, the Superior. Exalted is Allah above whatever they associate with Him."

(The Holy Quran 59:23)

Allah is the one who controls and protects everything in the universe. For example, if the earth would become a fraction closer to the sun it would burn and if it became a fraction further it would freeze. Everything is in His protection and mercy.

Keys to remember:

* Everything is under His control, no matter how strong or capable we may think we are, we can not do anything without his permission.

* His control over everything is amazing and it happens all the time even when we don't realize. For example, the human brain handles 10 quadrillion instructions per second in perfect harmony and precision under His control and all this goes on without us even realizing.

How this name effects my life:

_____
_____
_____
_____
_____
_____
_____

Al - 'Aziz

Al - 'Aziz

The Almighty, The Powerful. The Mighty. The Defeater who is not defeated.

" And to Allah belong the soldiers of the heavens and the earth. And ever is Allah Exalted in Might and Wise."
(The Holy Quran 48,7)

"Whatever is in the heavens and whatever is on the earth exalts Allah , and He is the Exalted in Might, the Wise."
(The Holy Quran 61,1)

Keys to remember:

- Allah is the almighty and the most powerful and being a true slave to Allah ensures that you will have this strength on your side. Allah has made humans the best of His creation and has made the believers the best of humans.
- Implement this name in your life by fearing no one but Him and always asking for His support and strength.

How this name effects my life:

_____

_____

_____

_____

_____

_____

_____

Al - Jabbaar

Al-Jabbaar,

The Compeller, The One that nothing happens in His Dominion except that which He willed.

There is also another meaning to this name which stems from the word "Jabr" in Arabic. The meaning of this word is to heal and mend something after it has been broken.
The word bandage in Arabic also stems from "Jabr" which is a perfect example of what this name of Allah means.

So if you feel your heart has been broken go to Al-Jabbar and with His will it will be mended and healed.

Keys to remember:

* On the Day of Judgment we will all be called by our names individually and told to come to stand in front of AlJabbar. This can feel extremely scary for us and also it can be comforting. Because while this name means complete dominion over everything, it also has another meaning which is the healer who fixes what has been broken.

* When you are hurt don't forget to call on Allah with this name to heal you.

How this name effects my life:

_____
_____
_____
_____
_____
_____
_____

Al - Mutakabir

Al-Mutakabir,

The Haughty, The Majestic. The Imperious. The Highest. The One who is clear from the attributes of the creatures and from resembling them.

Allah shows how great He is through many examples He gives in the Qur'an. For example,
"And when Moses arrived at Our appointed time and his Lord spoke to him, he said, "My Lord, show me [Yourself] that I may look at You." [Allah] said, "You will not see Me, but look at the mountain; if it should remain in place, then you will see Me." But when his Lord appeared to the mountain, He rendered it level, and Moses fell unconscious. And when he awoke, he said, "Exalted are You! I have repented to You, and I am the first of the believers."
(The Holy Quran 7,143)

Keys to remember:

★ Allah is the Highest above everything. He in no way resembles His creation. So we cannot compare Him to anything we know or see for He is far more superior.

★ Even though Allah is above us all He offers us His love and He informs us He is always with us, always seeing us and hearing us and answering our prayers. Even though He doesn't need us in any way , He is always there for us.

How this name effects my life:

_____
_____
_____
_____
_____
_____
_____

Al - Khaliq

Al-Khaliq,

The Creator, the Maker. The One who brings everything from non-existence to existence.

"O mankind, remember the favor of Allah upon you. Is there any creator other than Allah who provides for you from the heaven and earth? There is no deity except Him, so how are you deluded?"
The Holy Quran (35:3)

"That is Allah , your Lord; there is no deity except Him, the Creator of all things, so worship Him. And He is Disposer of all things."
The Holy Quran (6:102)

Keys to remember:

★ Every manufacturer has his signature or logo that shows a certain product is made by him and no one else. If you look at the universe and within yourself you will find that this holds true with Allah as well. If you look closely you will notice Allah's work and signature in everything around you. The precision, beauty and balance in His creation has no parallel.

How this name effects my life:

_____
_____
_____
_____
_____
_____
_____

Al - Baari'

البارئ

Al-Baari',

The Evolver, The Maker, The Creator who has the Power to turn the entities to what He wills.

"He is God, the Creator, the Maker who shapes all forms and appearances! His [alone] are the attributes of perfection. All that is in the heavens and on earth extols His limitless glory: for He alone is almighty, truly wise!"

(The Holy Quran 59:24)

Keys to remember:

★ Allah is the one and only one who can make anything He wants and change anything or any situation into what He wants. Never lose hope in Allah or His power no matter how bad the situation you are in is.

How this name effects my life:

_____
_____
_____
_____
_____
_____
_____

Al - Musawwir

المصور

Al-Musawwir,

The Organizer, The Designer, The Fashioner. The One who forms His creatures in different pictures.

One look at beautiful butterflies and the fantastic symmetry between its wings shows how Allah is the perfect Designer.

If we examine ourselves as humans and our complex and perfect structure, our bodies which perform thousands of complex operations every second we will realize how Allah is the greatest Designer and how He has formed us in the best of forms.

Keys to remember:

★ Allah has chosen humans to have the best of forms among all his creatures. He has honored us and elevated our status.

★ To appreciate this name of Allah make sure to practice the worship of tafakor "observance". Look at everything around you with deep appreciation of Allah's power and ability.

How this name effects my life:

_____
_____
_____
_____
_____
_____
_____

Al - Ghaffar

Al-Ghaffar

The Forgiving, The Forgiver. The One who forgives the sins of His slaves time and time again.

"Allah does not impose blame upon you for what is unintentional in your oaths, but He imposes blame upon you for what your hearts have earned. And Allah is Forgiving and Forbearing."
(The Holy Quran 2,225)

"And to Allah belongs whatever is in the heavens and whatever is on the earth. He forgives whom He wills and punishes whom He wills. And Allah is Forgiving and Merciful."
(The Holy Quran 3,129)

Keys to remember:

★ Sometimes we can stray from the path to Allah, and when we try to get back on the path, the devil makes us feel unworthy and that there is no hope for us. Especially if we commit the same sins many times, we lose hope that we will ever be any better and that Allah will ever forgive us. Allah called Himself the forgiver because He knows we will sin, but He promises us His forgiveness. No matter how far you think you are, run to Allah and He will guide you.

How this name effects my life:

_____
_____
_____
_____
_____
_____
_____

Al - Qahhaar

Al-Qahhaar

The Subduer, The Dominant, The One who has the perfect Power and is not unable over anything.

"For He alone holds sway over His creatures, and He alone is truly wise, all-aware."
                    The Holy Quran (6:18)

"[His promise will be fulfilled] on the Day when the earth shall be changed into another earth, as shall be the heavens [63] and when [all men] shall appear before God, the One who holds absolute sway over all that exists."
                    The Holy Quran (14:48)

Keys to remember:

★ Allah has complete power over us. Do not let your health, wealth, nice clothes, nice house....etc make you forget that. At the end us and everything around us comes under Allah's power. Never let pride enter your heart and make you think you have some power of your own.

How this name effects my life:

_____
_____
_____
_____
_____
_____
_____

Al - Wahhab

Al-Wahhab

The All and Ever Giving, The Bestower, The One who is Generous in giving plenty without any return.

"Our Lord, do not make our hearts swerve aside after You have guided us. And give us mercy from You. You are the Ever-Giving."
            The Holy Quran (3:8)

Everything we owe and posses is from Him. Every breath we take is a gift from Him. And for the believers He has prepared for them the best of gifts in the hereafter, paradise.

Keys to remember:

- As humans most of the time if not all the time when we give to others we always expect something in return. If we think we won't get anything in return most of the time we won't give in the first place. Allah on the other hand gives because He is the giver, He doesn't give because He wants something in return.
- Implement this name in your life by examining what Allah has given you with no return from you. You will find it countless and unmeasurable.

How this name effects my life:

_____
_____
_____
_____
_____
_____
_____

Ar - Razzaaq

Ar-Razzaaq,

The Sustainer, The Provider.

"Indeed, it is Allah who is the [continual] Provider, the firm possessor of strength."

(The Holy Quran 51,58)

"And whoever fears Allah - He will make for him a way out - And will provide for him from where he does not expect. And whoever relies upon Allah - then He is sufficient for him. Indeed, Allah will accomplish His purpose. Allah has already set for everything a [decreed] extent."

(The Holy Quran 65,2-3)

Keys to remember:

★ Our sustenance comes from Allah and Allah alone. Unfortunately sometimes we forget that and tie our sustenance to a certain person or a certain job..etc. This can lead us to do things that are against our faith and Allah because we forget that Allah is the One who provides for us all the time.

★ Our rizk (sustenance) has many forms, it is not only money. It can be good health, family, friends, nice place to live, inner peace...etc.

How this name effects my life:

_____

_____

_____

_____

_____

_____

_____

Al - Fattaah

Al-Fattaah,

The Opener, The Reliever, The One who opens for His slaves the closed worldly and religious matters.

Allah tests us in life with hardships and trials. But no matter how difficult these trials become Allah will always open a way out for the believer. When you are distressed and not sure how to get out of a situation ask Allah with his name Al-Fattah to open all closed doors for you.

"Our Sustainer will bring us all together [on Judgment Day], and then He will lay open the truth between us, in justice - for He alone is the One who opens all truth, the All-Knowing!"

(The Holy Quran 34:26)

Keys to remember:

★ He is the opener of all closed doors, so never give up. If you want to do something that is halal that will benefit you then never lose hope that Allah will make it work.

★ Implement this name in your life by making dua'a to Allah using this name. Ask Him on a daily basis to open up everything for you and make all hardships easier using this name.

How this name effects my life:

_____
_____
_____
_____
_____
_____
_____

Al - 'Alim

Al - 'Alim

The all Knowing, The Omniscient, The Knowledgeable; The One nothing is absent from His knowledge.

"Both East and West belong to Allah, so wherever you turn, the Face of Allah is there. Allah is All-Encompassing, All-Knowing."
             The Holy Quran (2:115)

"He it is who has created for you all that is on earth, and has applied His design to the heavens and fashioned them into seven heavens; and He alone has full knowledge of everything."
             The Holy Quran (2:29)

Allah has complete knowledge of everything in the universe regardless of time and space. He also knows our secrets and our inner thoughts. His knowledge is boundless.

Keys to remember:

★ Nothing escapes Allah's knowledge. He knows you more than anyone ever will. So trust in Him that He knows all your suffering, desires and hopes. He is closer to you than your jugular vain.

★ Implement this name in your life by making dua'a to Allah asking Him to give you from His knowledge that is beneficial for you in this life and the next.

How this name effects my life:

_____

_____

_____

_____

_____

_____

_____

Al - Qabed

Al - Qabed,

The Contractor, The Restrainer. The One who constricts the sustenance.

"Allah extends provision for whom He wills of His servants and restricts for whom He wills. Indeed Allah is, of all things, Knowing."
(The Holy Quran 29,62)

"Do they not see that Allah extends provision for whom He wills and restricts [it]? Indeed, in that are signs for a people who believe."
(The Holy Quran 30,37)

Keys to remember:

★ Allah both gives and constricts sustenance but this is not an indicator if Allah loves someone or not or is happy with someone or not. Allah may constrict the sustenance of a Muslim because this is better for him and He may give to a non Muslim because he takes his reward in this life as he will receive nothing in the next.

How this name effects my life:

_____
_____
_____
_____
_____
_____
_____

Al - Basit

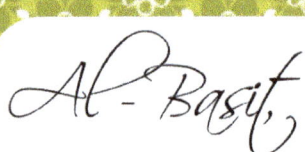

The Expander, He who expands. The One who expands and widens and gives abundantly.

" Who is it that will offer up unto God a goodly loan, [234] which He will amply repay, with manifold increase? For, God takes away, and He gives abundantly; and it is unto Him that you shall be brought back."

(The Holy Quran 2,245)

"God grants abundant sustenance, or gives it in scant measure, unto whomever He wills; and they [who are given abundance] rejoice in the life of this world - even though, as compared with the life to come, the life of this world is nothing but -a fleeting pleasure."

(The Holy Quran 13,26)

Keys to remember:

* As humans it is very hard for us to give without getting nothing in return even if it's just the love of the other person. On the other hand, Allah gives us all the time in abundance without asking for something in return.
* If a door of sustenance (rizq) is opened for us widely, we always need to be careful that it is something pleasing to Allah. All the world's treasures are worth nothing if Allah is angry with us.

How this name effects my life:

_____
_____
_____
_____
_____
_____
_____

Al - Khafed

الفاخض

Al - Khafed,

The Abaser, the Humbler. The One who lowers whoever He wills by His Destruction.

" When the Occurrence occurs,There is, at its occurrence, no denial.It will bring down [some] and raise up [others]."
(The Holy Quran 56:1,2,3)

"We have certainly created man in the best of stature;Then We return him to the lowest of the low,Except for those who believe and do righteous deeds, for they will have a reward uninterrupted."
(The Holy Quran 9:4,5,6)

Keys to remember:

- ★ Pride is a terrible disease that sadly afflicts many of us. Even though in reality we have no true power or control over anything. If Allah decrees we can lose our health and all our wealth in a blink of an eye.

- ★ To implement this name in our lives we should always be humble with our dealings with Allah and with other people.

How this name effects my life:

_____
_____
_____
_____
_____
_____
_____

Ar - Rafi'

الرافع

Ar-Rafi'

The Raiser, the Exalter. The One who raises whoever He willed by His Endowment.

"Mention Idris in the Book. He was a true man and a Prophet. We raised him up to a high place."
                              The Holy Quran (19:56-57)

Those who believe in Allah and follow the straight path, Allah will raise their status in this life and the next.

Keys to remember:

★ We all wish to be respected and put in high regard by people, the right way to get that is by following the straight path. We should not care about what people think, instead we should live to please Allah and as a reward Allah we elevate our status in this life and the next.

How this name effects my life:

_____
_____
_____
_____
_____
_____
_____

Al - Mu'z

Al-Mu'z

The Honorer, the Exalter. He gives esteem to whoever He wills.

"Say: O Allah! Owner of Sovereignty! You give sovereignty unto whom You will, and You withdraw sovereignty from whom You will; You exalt whom You will, and You abase whom You will. In Your hand is the good. Lo! You are Able to do all things; You are Possessor of power over all things." (The Holy Quran 3:26)

"Those who take disbelievers for Auliya (protectors or helpers or friends) instead of believers, do they seek honour, power and glory with them? Verily, then to Allah belongs all honour, power and glory." (The Holy Quran 4:139)

Keys to remember:

★ Allah gives honour and esteem to whoever He wishes. It is important here to note that honour in the sight of Allah can be different than the honour in the sight of people. For example, many people who spread evil and are sinners are often given false honour and status such as movie stars and singers...etc. On the other hand there are sincere devout believers who are not known to people but they have true honour in the sight of Allah.

How this name effects my life:

_____
_____
_____
_____
_____
_____
_____

Al - Muzil

Al-Muzil

The Abaser, The Degrader, The Humiliator, He Degrades whoever He wills.

Allah humiliates the un-believers and those who turn away from His message as a punishment in both this world and the next.

"You may travel about in the land for four months and know that you cannot thwart Allah, and that Allah will humiliate the unbelievers."

(The Holy Quran 9:2)

Keys to remember:

* Allah's commandments are for our best so we can live a decent, happy and fulfilling life and to help us reach paradise. The people who refuse to follow Allah's path are degraded both in this life and the next even if they do not realize. For instance, look at the people who get drunk with alcohol and how they commit disgusting acts while under the influence. They humiliate themselves by not following Allah's commands.

How this name effects my life:

_____

_____

_____

_____

_____

_____

Al - Sami'

As-Sami',

The All-Hearing, The Hearer, The One who Hears all things that are heard by His Eternal Hearing without an ear, instrument or organ.

"Say, "If I should err, I would only err against myself. But if I am guided, it is by what my Lord reveals to me. Indeed, He is Hearing and near.""

(The Holy Quran 34,50)

"[He is] Creator of the heavens and the earth. He has made for you from yourselves, mates, and among the cattle, mates; He multiplies you thereby. There is nothing like unto Him, and He is the Hearing, the Seeing."

(The Holy Quran 42,11)

Keys to remember:

★ We all know that Allah hears us at all times and at all places but sometimes when we are going through difficult times we forget to actually connect with Him. Instead of complaining to people all the time go to Allah and talk to Him. He hears you and is waiting for you. Talk to Him in the language that makes you comfortable and trust He will listen to you.

How this name effects my life:

_____

_____

_____

_____

_____

_____

_____

Al - Baseer

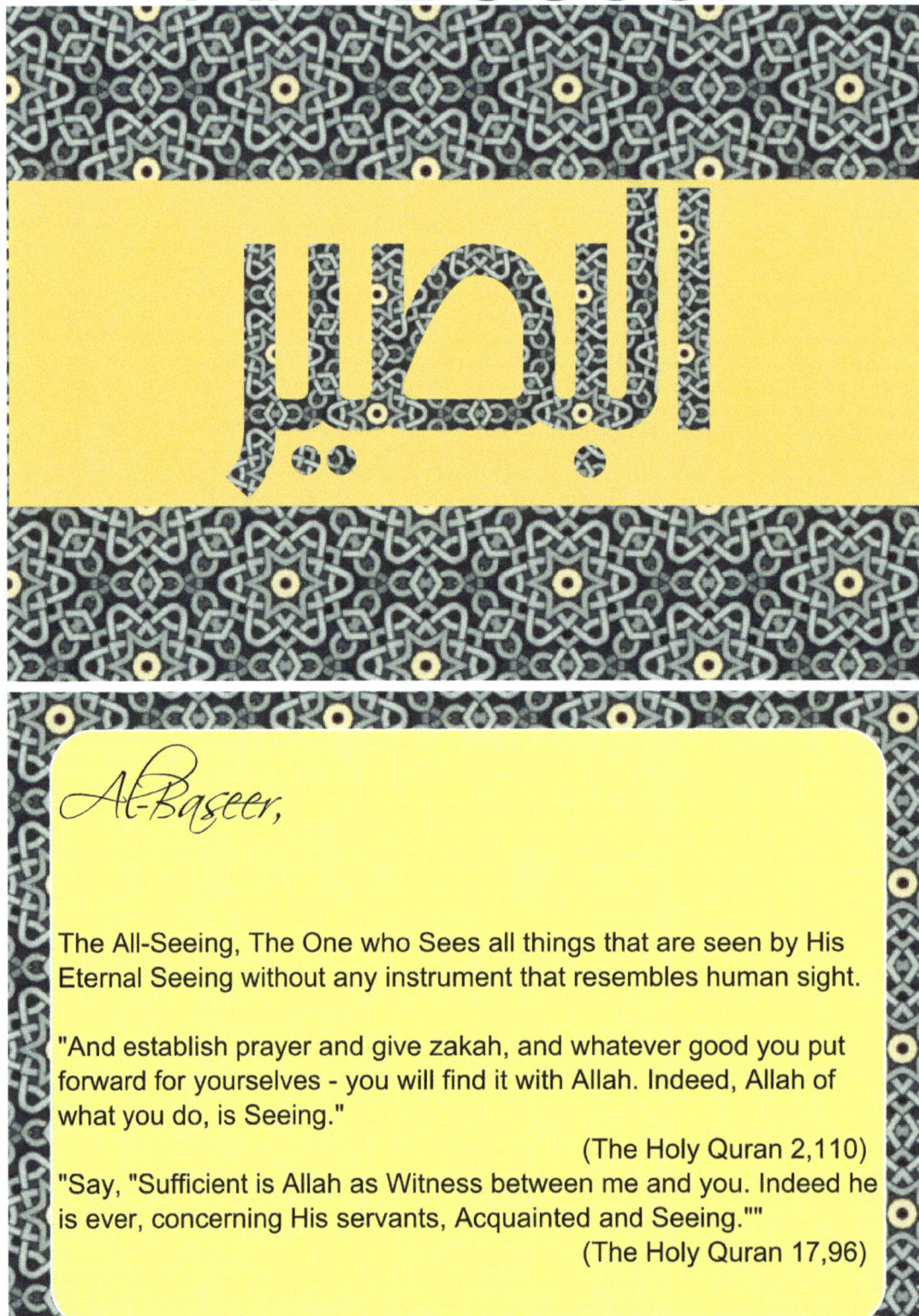

Al-Baseer,

The All-Seeing, The One who Sees all things that are seen by His Eternal Seeing without any instrument that resembles human sight.

"And establish prayer and give zakah, and whatever good you put forward for yourselves - you will find it with Allah. Indeed, Allah of what you do, is Seeing."

(The Holy Quran 2,110)

"Say, "Sufficient is Allah as Witness between me and you. Indeed he is ever, concerning His servants, Acquainted and Seeing.""

(The Holy Quran 17,96)

Keys to remember:

★ We naturally care about what people think of us and how they see us. We can spend hours beautifying ourselves in front of a mirror to get people's approval. We need not to forget that Allah sees us at all times but Allah is not concerned with our outward looks. Allah is concerned with our hearts. We need to purify our hearts constantly and renew our intentions. We should also ask Allah to make our hearts as He pleases.

How this name effects my life:

_____
_____
_____
_____
_____
_____

Al - Hakam

الحكم

Al-Hakam

The Arbitrator, The Judge. He is the Ruler and His judgment is His Word.

"And follow what is revealed to you, [O Muhammad], and be patient until Allah will judge. And He is the best of judges." (The Holy Quran 10:109)

The day will come when we will stand between His hands to be judged on everything we did in this life. Make sure to prepare for this day.

Keys to remember:

★ In this world there is a lot of injustice and we might not be able to get our rights back from a human judge. But never forget that the true judgment will be when Allah judges between everyone with complete justice. So make sure to both be ready for that day and never to despair if you encounter injustice.

How this name effects my life:

_____
_____
_____
_____
_____
_____
_____

Al - 'Adl

Al-'Adl

The Justice, The Equitable, The Just.

Allah is the most Just. He treats us all with complete justice. Nothing escapes His knowledge and His justice. On the Day of Judgement we will all be judged with complete justice.

"On the Day We summon every people with their records, those who are given their Book in their right hand will read their Book and will not be wronged by even the smallest speck."
(The Holy Quran 17:71)

Allah also commands us to be just in all our dealings without being bias to anyone for any reason.

Keys to remember:

* When we think of Allah's justice we need to remember that it's not only related to Allah's judgment between us. Allah is just in all His dealings with us and with all the sustenance He provides for us. If you find yourself feeling envious or jealous towards someone who seems to have more than you, remind yourself that Allah is just and gives us all with His wisdom. Never doubt Allah's justice and know that Allah always gives us the best.

How this name effects my life:

_____

_____

_____

_____

_____

_____

_____

Al - Latif

The Most Gentle, The Gracious. The One who is kind

"Do you not see that Allah has sent down rain from the sky and the earth becomes green? Indeed, Allah is The Most Gentle and All-aware."   The Holy Quran (22:63)

"Allah is most kind unto His creatures: He provides sustenance for whomever He wills - for He alone is powerful, almighty!"   The Holy Quran (42:19)

No one loves you more than Allah does so go to Him and trust in Him.

Keys to remember:

★ You will never find anyone kinder to you than Allah himself. No one can love you and want the best for you more than Allah. Do not let anything take you away from this beautiful relationship from Allah. When you are sad or feeling down never forget that Allah is there for you and in fact He is the only one who can heal your heart.

How this name effects my life:

_____

_____

_____

_____

_____

_____

_____

Al - Khabir

Al-Khabir,

The All Aware. The One who knows the truth of things.

"And He is the subjugator over His servants. And He is the Wise, the Aware [with all]." (The Holy Quran 6:18)

"O mankind, indeed We have created you from male and female and made you peoples and tribes that you may know one another. Indeed, the most noble of you in the sight of Allah is the most righteous of you. Indeed, Allah is Knowing and Acquainted." (The Holy Quran 49:13)

Keys to remember:

* Allah knows you more than anyone else. What you can hide from people you cannot hide from Allah. Remember to always purify your intentions and make all your deeds for Allah only. If you do something for people to think good of you and not for the sake of Allah then you will not gain the reward. So make it a point to always check your intentions at all times.

How this name effects my life:

_____

_____

_____

_____

_____

_____

_____

Al - Halim

Al-Halim

The Gentle. The most patient, the forbearing, the Clement. The One who delays the punishment for those who deserve it and then He might forgive them.

"Verily, it is God [alone] who upholds the celestial bodies and the earth, lest they deviate [from their orbits] - for if they should ever deviate, there is none that could uphold them after He will have ceased to do so. [But,] verily, He is ever-forbearing, much-forgiving"

The Holy Quran (3:8)

Allah is the most patient and forbearing, He does not punish us for our sins right away, He gives us chance after chance. The same applies even with the unbelievers. When we do a good deed it is counted as 10 and maybe more but when we do a bad deed it is only counted as one.

Keys to remember:

★ We can lose people in our lives even if we love them very much because of disputes or disagreements, differences...etc. But Allah is the most gentle and He is always there for us no matter what. Allah is very patient with us and even if we feel at times we get very far from Him we should never feel that we are too far to get close to Him again.

How this name effects my life:

_____
_____
_____
_____
_____
_____

Al - 'Azim

Al-'Azim

The Great, ,The Glorious, The Mighty, The One deserving the attributes of Exaltment, Glory, and Purity from all imperfection.

Allah's grandeur is beyond our capacity to comprehend. But we can get close to realizing how great He must be if we examine the universe we live in. We live in an open ended space which contains billions of galaxies with countless billions of stars.
We live in one of these galaxies on one of its planets. In comparison to this huge universe we are as small as the existence of a dust particle on Earth. And all of these billions of galaxies in comparison to Allah's greatness are also no more than a particle of dust or less.

Keys to remember:

* No matter how big your dreams are or how big the obstacles you face in life, remember that Allah is greater than everything and anything in this world. His greatness is beyond our comprehension, not only is that evident in His creation but also in how Allah deals with us and how much He loves us, forgives us, always hears us and is always there for us.

How this name effects my life:

_____
_____
_____
_____
_____
_____
_____

Al - Ghafoor

Al-Ghafoor,

The Forgiving, The Pardoner. The One who forgives a lot.

Say [O Prophet]: "If you love God, follow me, [and] God will love you and forgive you your sins; for God is much-Forgiving, a dispenser of grace."

(The Holy Quran 3:31)

"And to Allah belongs whatever is in the heavens and whatever is on the earth. He forgives whom He wills and punishes whom He wills. And Allah is Forgiving and Merciful."

(The Holy Quran 3:129)

Keys to remember:

★ Allah loves you. No matter where you have been, no matter what you have done, no matter how deep you have fell; there is always forgiveness. The only thing you have to worry about is repentess. If you are guided to repent from sin than Allah willing He will forgive you.

★ To truly repent, you need to stop the sin, intend never to repeat it and ask Allah to forgive you. A good practice after commiting a sin is doing an extra good deed after it so hopefully it replaces the bad deed.

How this name effects my life:

_____

_____

_____

_____

_____

_____

_____

Al - Shakur

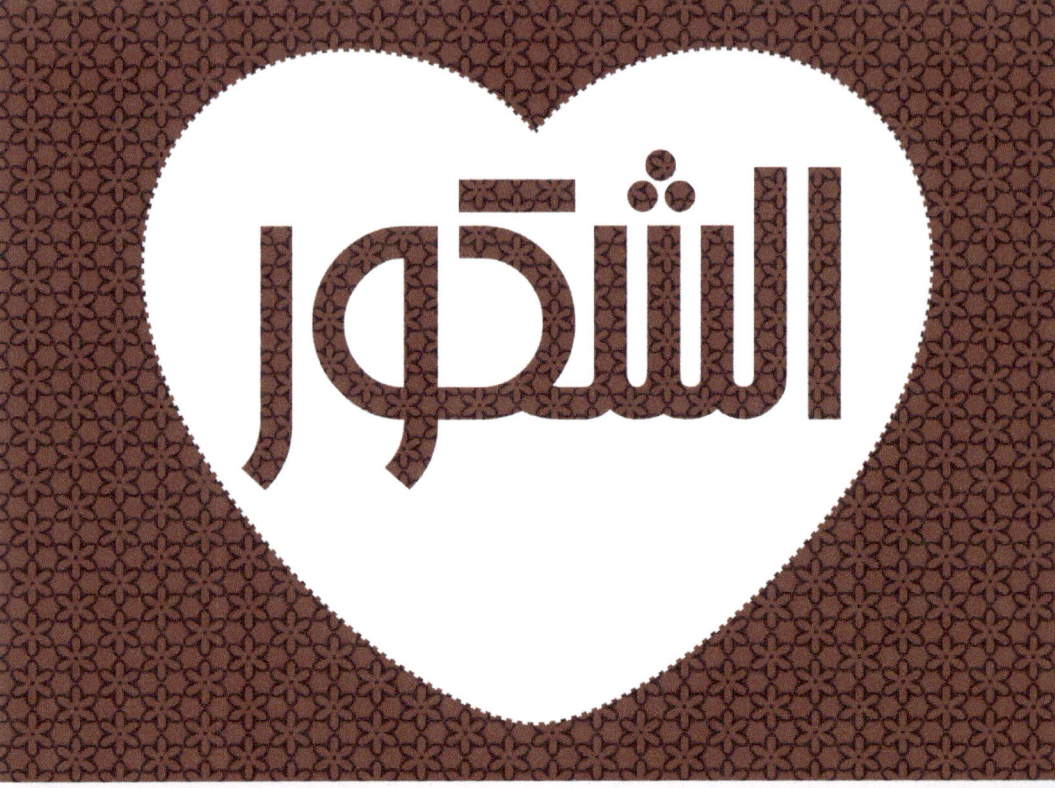

Al - Shakur,

The Rewarder of Thankfulness, The Appreciative. The One who gives a lot of reward for ittle obedience.

"And they will say, "Praise to Allah, who has removed from us [all] sorrow. Indeed, our Lord is Forgiving and Appreciative"
(The Holy Quran 35:34)

"It is that of which Allah gives good tidings to His servants who believe and do righteous deeds. Say, [O Muhammad], "I do not ask you for this message any payment [but] only good will through kinship." And whoever commits a good deed - We will increase for him good therein. Indeed, Allah is Forgiving and Appreciative."
(The Holy Quran 42:23)

Keys to remember:

★ People may forget the good you do for them but Allah never forgets. Anything you do no matter how small you will be rewarded for. So make sure to try and always purify your intentions in anything you do and make it for the sake of Allah.

★ Allah shows His love for us in how He rewards us. For every 1 good deed we do we get 10 rewards. If Allah treated us with only justice and not extreme mercy we would only get 1 reward not 10.

How this name effects my life:

_____
_____
_____
_____
_____
_____
_____

Al - 'Ali

Al-'Ali

The Most High, The Exalted. The One who is clear from the attributes of the creatures.

"Thus it is, because God alone is the Ultimate Truth, so that all that men invoke beside Him is sheer falsehood, and because God alone is Exalted, and Great."
					The Holy Quran (22:62)

"To Him belongs whatever is in the heavens and whatever is in the earth, and He is the Most High, the Most Great."
					The Holy Quran (42:4)

Keys to remember:

★ When we think of Allah we need to realize that He doesn't resemble anything we have ever seen or heard before. He is higher than everything we know as we are merely His creation. We should keep this in mind when we are worshipping Him to help us in trying to imrpove our worship as much as possible. For example in prayer, we should try and focus and fill our heart with Allah alone and how great He is.

How this name effects my life:

_____

_____

_____

_____

_____

_____

Al - Kabir

Al-Kabir,

The Great, The Grand, The Big, The One who is greater than everything else.

"[He is] Knower of the unseen and the witnessed, the Grand, the Exalted." (The Holy Quran 13:9)

"That is because Allah is the Truth, and that which they call upon other than Him is falsehood, and because Allah is the Most High, the Grand." (The Holy Quran 22:62)

Do not be decieved by this world there is nothing or anyone greater than Him. Do not rely upon anything else but Him.

Keys to remember:

★ How beautiful is it when you are hurt or lost not knowing what to do or where to go that you can run to the Greatest! The one who is greater than anyone or anything. No matter how great your problems are Allah is greater.

How this name effects my life:

_____
_____
_____
_____
_____
_____
_____

Al - Hafiz

Al - Hafiz

The Guardian, the preserver. The One who protects whatever and whoever He wills to protect.

"And yet, he [the devil] had no power at all over them: [for if We allow him to tempt man,] it is only to the end that We might make a clear distinction between those who [truly] believe in the life to come and those who are in doubt thereof: And your Lord, over all things, is Guardian."

The Holy Quran (34:21)

The Prophet (peace and blessings be upon him) said:
"Be mindful of Allah and He will protect you. Be mindful of Allah, and you will find Him in front of you."

Hadith at-Tirmidhi - Hasan Sahih

Keys to remember:

★ We live in times that leave us seeking protection more than ever. It is important to take worldly measures to protect ourselves but ultimately true protection comes from Allah. So never forget to seek His protection at all times.

★ Not only do we need protection from external threats but we also need protection from ourselves. Our own desires may lead us astray and cause us harm. We need to ask Allah's protection from everything that can harm us including ourselves.

How this name effects my life:

_____
_____
_____
_____
_____
_____
_____

Al - Muqit

Al-Muqit

The Maintainer, The Nourisher. The One who has the Power.

"He placed therein (the earth) firm mountains from above it and He blessed it and measured therein its sustenance (food for its dwellers) in four Days equal for all those who ask (about creation)."
(The Holy Quran 41:10)

Allah is the one who creates all the bodily and spiritual nourishment such as food and beverage, science and knowledge, with which He maintains the faculties of all living things and grants them what suffices the existence of their bodies. Allah's name Al - Muqit also denotes that He overwhelms everything with His Power and is responsible for all things with His comprehensive and all-inclusive Knowledge.

Keys to remember:

★ Allah gives us what we need to survive and what is best for us in the way that is best for us. We may forget in the midst of our busy lives that it is indeed Allah who is providing for us at all times. His sustenance for us includes everything in our lives whether it is our relationships, our health, or even daylight for us to be able to perform our daily affairs.

How this name effects my life:

_____

_____

_____

_____

_____

_____

_____

Al - Haseeb

Al-Haseeb,

The Reckoner, The One who keeps count of all things.

But when you are greeted with a greeting [of peace], answer with an even better greeting, or [at least] with the like thereof. Verily, God keeps count indeed of all things.
(The Holy Quran 4:86)

As humans we easily forget things we did in the past and experiences we had. So much so that years of our life are limited to vague and dim memories. However, this is not the case with Allah who takes account of everything and will recount all of our deeds to us on the Day of Judgment.

Keys to remember:

★ It is both intimidating and comforting that Allah keeps count of everything no matter how small. Try to remember Allah in any action you take no matter how small or mundane. Put an intention in all deeds you do even sleeping or eating. For example, when you sleep make an intention you're doing it to gain energy to be able to worship Allah and perform your worldly duties and Allah willing you will gain rewards even while sleeping.

How this name effects my life:

_____

_____

_____

_____

_____

_____

_____

Al - Jalil

The Majestic. The Honorable, The Exalted. The One who is attributed with greatness of Power and Glory of status.

Allah, the Creator of all the worlds and the sole Sovereign of the universe, is the Most Honorable and the Possessor of the heavens, Earth, and everything in between. There is no deity but Him.

All of the beautiful names belong to Allah, for He is the most Majestic and Exalted.

Keys to remember:

★ Allah is the most Honorable and the possessor of everything. He has no need for us or our worship. It is Allah's mercy that He has given humans such a high status on earth above all other creations. It is also a blessing to us and a true honor that He allows us to worship Him. We should never feel that worshiping Him is a favor from us, in fact it's a huge blessing that we should thank Allah for.

How this name effects my life:

_____

_____

_____

_____

_____

_____

_____

Al - Kareem

Al-Kareem

The Most Generous, The Bountiful.

".....And whoever is grateful - his gratitude is only for [the benefit of] himself. And whoever is ungrateful - then indeed, my Lord is Free of need and Generous."

(The Holy Quran 27:40)

Allah is The Most Generous, unlike humans He likes to be called upon and asked. He likes to hear the voice of His slaves asking from Him and gets angry when they don't. Always ask Allah to give you what you want and need no matter how small. He is more generous than we can imagine.

Keys to remember:

★ Allah's generosity has no bounds. He gives us without us even asking, so can you imagine what He will give you if you go to Him and ask?

★ Always go to Allah and ask from Him, nothing is too big for Allah to give you, the whole universe is in His command.

How this name effects my life:

_____
_____
_____
_____
_____
_____
_____

Ar - Raqib

Ar-Raqib,

The Guardian, TheWatcher, The One that nothing is absent from Him. Hence it's meaning is related to the attribute of Knowledge.

"...And remain conscious of God, in whose name you demand [your rights] from one another, and of these ties of kinship. Verily, God is ever watchful over you!"   The Holy Quran (4:1)

Allah protects and watches all beings from the galaxies and stars to the humans and other creatures on this planet. Nothing we do escapes His knowledge. We always need to be mindful before taking any action that He watches everything we do and all our deeds should be to please Him.

Keys to remember:

- ★ He is always there watching us in everything we do. This should bring us comfort as He knows all what we go through and all good we do. At the same time we need to be mindful of our actions, even if no one else knows what we do Allah always will.

How this name effects my life:

_____
_____
_____
_____
_____
_____
_____

Al - Mujib

Al-Mujib,

The Responder. The respondent one who answers. The One who answers the one in need if he asks Him and rescues his slave if he calls upon Him.

"And if My servants ask you about Me - behold, I am near; I respond to the call of him who calls, whenever he calls unto Me: let them, then, respond unto Me, and believe in Me, so that they might follow the right way." (The Holy Quran 2:186)

When you pray to Allah asking for something lawful, Allah responds in three ways. He will either give you what you asked for, or give you something else that is better for you, or protect you from something evil that would have befallen you.

Keys to remember:

- ★ Allah likes us to ask from Him and in fact gets angry if we don't. There are many special times that Allah made for us to increase the chance of our prayers being accepted. Some for example are: the last third of the night, in prostration during prayer, between the two calls for prayer, at the breaking of our fast...etc.
- ★ Ask Allah in all your affairs no matter how small and Allah willing you will have a wonderful relationship with Him.

How this name effects my life:

_____
_____
_____
_____
_____
_____
_____

Al - Wasi'

الواسع

Al-Wasi',

The All-Encompassing, The Vast, The All-Embracing, The Knowledgeable.

"And to Allah belongs the east and the west. So wherever you [might] turn, there is the Face of Allah . Indeed, Allah is all-Encompassing and Knowing."

(The Holy Quran 2:115)

"The example of those who spend their wealth in the way of Allah is like a seed [of grain] which grows seven spikes; in each spike is a hundred grains. And Allah multiplies [His reward] for whom He wills. And Allah is all-Encompassing and Knowing."

(The Holy Quran 2:261)

Keys to remember:

* As humans our knowledge, ability, strength...etc is limited and compared to Allah all our abilities in fact mount to nothing. This is why we should always trust in Allah and how He has decreed our life to be. We can never know the wisdom behind everything in this life but we trust that Allah does, so we submit to Him.

How this name effects my life:

_____
_____
_____
_____
_____
_____
_____

Al - Hakim

The most Wise, The Judicious. The One who is correct in His doings.

"For He alone holds sway over His creatures, and He alone is truly wise, All-Aware."
(The Holy Quran 6:18)

"Falsehood cannot approach it from before it or from behind it; [it is] a revelation from a [Lord who is] Wise and Praiseworthy."
(The Holy Quran 41:42)

Keys to remember:

★ Nothing happens in this world except with Allah's wisdom. Even if we can't understand why things happen the way they do, we need to trust in Allah's wisdom. More often than not even if we don't understand the reasoning at the time usually later on in life we can look back and see the wisdom behind it.

★ Allah's wisdom in not limited to His decree for us but also in His commandments. There is always wisdom behind what He ordains for us.

How this name effects my life:

_____
_____
_____
_____
_____
_____
_____

Al - Wadud

الودود

Al-Wadud,

The Loving, The Kind One. The One who is with High Status, Compassion, Generosity and Kindness.

"And ask forgiveness of your Lord and then repent to Him. Indeed, my Lord is Merciful and Affectionate."
(The Holy Quran 11:90)

"And He is the Forgiving, the Affectionate."
(The Holy Quran 85:14)

Keys to remember:

★ Yearning for love? We all are. There is no greater love than the love of Allah himself. If you truly feel Allah's love for you, you will be filled with indescribable joy that nothing else in this world can come close to.

★ Allah shows His love to us through action, He gives us everything we have in life. He forgives us, is merciful with us, made paradise for us and so much more. We too should express our love for Allah in action. Saying it is not enough, we need to prove our love for Allah by doing what pleases Him and staying away from what doesn't.

How this name effects my life:

_____

_____

_____

_____

_____

_____

Al - Majeed

Al-Majeed,

The Glorious, the exalted. The One who is with perfect Power, High Status, Compassion, Generosity and Kindness.

"They said: Wonder you at Allah's commandment? The mercy of Allah and His blessings on you, O people of the house! Surely He is Praised, Glorious."
(The Holy Quran 11:73)

"And there will remain the Face of your Lord, Owner of Majesty and Honor."
(The Holy Quran 55:27)

Keys to remember:

★ Allah is perfect in every way, something as humans it is very hard for us to imagine and impossible to ever implement. That is why it is important for us to put our trust in Him, He will never let us down if we do. He may test us in hard ways but He does it for our benefit. At the end, this life is very insignificant compared to our everlasting one.

How this name effects my life:

_____
_____
_____
_____
_____
_____
_____

Al - Ba'ith

Al - Ba'ith

The Resurrector, The Raiser from death. The One who resurrects for reward and/or punishment.

"That is because Allah is the Truth and because He gives life to the dead and because He is over all things competent"
(The Holy Quran 22:6)

"And [that they may know] that the Hour is coming - no doubt about it - and that Allah will resurrect those in the graves."
(The Holy Quran 22:7)

Keys to remember:

* The only fact in life that we can all guarantee without a shadow of doubt is that our lives will come to an end and we will stand in front of Allah. To understand our purpose in life and to not lose direction it's important we remember this fact. No matter what we achieve in this life, at the end, the only thing that will matter is what we have done for the next one.

How this name effects my life:

___
___
___
___
___
___
___

Ash - Shaheed

Ash -Shaheed,

The Witness. The One who nothing is absent from Him.

"Say, "O People of the Scripture, why do you disbelieve in the verses of Allah while Allah is Witness over what you do?""
(The Holy Quran 3,98)

"But Allah bears witness to that which He has revealed to you. He has sent it down with His knowledge, and the angels bear witness [as well]. And sufficient is Allah as Witness."
(The Holy Quran 4,166)

Keys to remember:

* When you are in doubt of what to do in any situation, remember Allah is witnessing it. If you are not sure if something you are doing is good or bad, think to yourself do I really want Allah to see me doing this? If you do this as much as possible, it will help you stay on the straight path.

How this name effects my life:

_____
_____
_____
_____
_____
_____
_____

Al - Haqq

Al - Haqq,

The Truth.

"Then they His servants are returned to Allah , their true Lord. Unquestionably, His is the judgment, and He is the swiftest of accountants."

(The Holy Quran 6,62)

"That is because Allah is the Truth and because He gives life to the dead and because He is over all things competent"

(The Holy Quran 22,6)

"Know then, [that] God is sublimely exalted, the Ultimate Sovereign, the Ultimate Truth: there is no deity save Him, the Sustainer, in bountiful almightiness enthroned! "

(The Holy Quran 23,116)

Keys to remember:

* Allah is the ultimate truth of this world, He created us and everything else. Some people go astray by thinking that to know something and admit its true existence they need to feel, touch, smell or see it. When it comes to knowing the truth of Allah we can do that by observing His creation with our senses, we don't need to see Allah himself. The truth is clear for anyone who doesn't turn away from it. For example, can you imagine a complete junk yard full of broken car pieces and suddenly a wind comes from no-where and just blows through the junk and rubbish and out of that a brand new working car is made? It doesn't make any sense, just as those who claim that this perfect universe came into existence by coincidence and chaos.

How this name effects my life:

_____

_____

_____

_____

Al - Wakil

الوكيل

Al-Wakil

The Guardian, the ultimate Trustee. The One who is relied upon.

"Those to whom hypocrites said, "Indeed, the people have gathered against you, so fear them." But it [merely] increased them in faith, and they said, "Sufficient for us is Allah , and [He is] the best Disposer of affairs and the Trustee.""
(The Holy Quran 3:137)

"And to Allah belongs whatever is in the heavens and whatever is on the earth. And sufficient is Allah as Disposer of affairs."
(The Holy Quran 4:132)

Keys to remember:

★ Sometimes you need others to carry out affairs on your behalf. So you choose someone you trust and give them the legal right to carry out your affairs. But how many times has it happened to you or others where people have betrayed that trust? Or that maybe they were trustworthy but didn't have the proper ability to help you in the best way. What if you handed over your affairs to the ultimate trustee? The only one who you can fully trust without hesitation and the only one who will never let you down.

How this name effects my life:

_____
_____
_____
_____
_____
_____

Al - Qawee

الْقَوِيُّ

Al-Qawee,

The Powerful, the Almighty, the Strong. The One with the complete Power.

"They have not appraised Allah with true appraisal. Indeed, Allah is Powerful and Exalted in Might."
(The Holy Quran 22:74)

"Allah has written, "I will surely overcome, I and My messengers." Indeed, Allah is Powerful and Exalted in Might."
(The Holy Quran 58:21)

Keys to remember:

★ Don't let any apparent strength you have fool you. As humans we go through ups and downs of strength all our lives and at the end we lose it all. That includes both mental and physical strength. The only strength that is the same, never changes and is always there is Allah's strength. No matter how strong someone thinks they are and may even use their strength to intimidate others, at the of the day it will all become just part of history.

★ Ask Allah to protect you with His strength from your weakness.

How this name effects my life:

_____

_____

_____

_____

_____

_____

Al - Matin

Al-Matin

The Strong, the Firm. The One with extreme Power which is uninterrupted and He does not get tired.

"Indeed, it is Allah who is the [continual] Provider, the firm possessor of strength."

(The Holy Quran 51,58)

Allah is the possessor of strength, any strength we may have in this world is a blessing from Him. Our strength is only temporary and in comparison to Allah's strength it is equal to nothing. We need to turn to Him in submission and obedience and believe that whatever He wills will take place and whatever He doesn't won't.

Keys to remember:

★ Who can you rely on to be there for you all the time no matter what? Who can you rely on to always give you what you need when you need it? Who can you rely on to give you what is best for you even if it's not what you want. The answer: Allah the most powerful, is the only one you can truly rely on with no limitations at all.

How this name effects my life:

_____
_____
_____
_____
_____
_____

Al - Wali

Al-Wali

The Protector, The Ally, The Supporter, The Helper.

"Your ally is none but Allah and [therefore] His Messenger and those who have believed - those who establish prayer and give zakah, and they bow [in worship]."
(The Holy Quran 5,55)

"And it is He who sends down the rain after they had despaired and spreads His mercy. And He is the Protector, the Praiseworthy."
(The Holy Quran 42,28)

Keys to remember:

★ How beautiful is it to the have the strongest, wisest, most capable, most loving one ever as your ally? How safe, content and happy would you be? In fact nothing can bring peace and calmness to your heart like having Him on your side.

★ Allah is the ally and supporter of the believers. Nothing in this world is more precious than to have Him as your ally. Make sure not to waste this beautiful relationship for anything trivial in this world.

How this name effects my life:

_____
_____
_____
_____
_____
_____

Al - Hamid

Al - Hamid

The Praiseworthy, The Commendable. The praised One who deserves to be praised.

"Alif, Lam, Ra. [This is] a Book which We have revealed to you, [O Muhammad], that you might bring mankind out of darkness into the light by permission of their Lord - to the path of the Exalted in Might, the Praiseworthy."

(The Holy Quran 14,1)

"To Him belongs what is in the heavens and what is on the earth. And indeed, Allah is the Free of need, the Praiseworthy."

(The Holy Quran 22,64)

Keys to remember:

★ When someone does one nice thing for you to make you happy you feel so grateful and make sure to thank that person. And most likely if you treat someone in a bad manner and are ungrateful for what they do for you, you will lose your relationship with that person. Allah gives us absolutely everything we have regardless of our sins and shortcomings. No matter what we do we can never thank Him enough. Indeed He is the praiseworthy, we should praise Him and thank Him day and night.

How this name effects my life:

_____
_____
_____
_____
_____
_____
_____

Al - Muhsi

Al-Mushi,

The Counter. The One who keeps the account of all things.

"That He may know that they have truly delivered the messages of their Lord; and He encompasses what is with them, and He keeps account of all things."
(The Holy Quran 72:28)

"He has counted them and numbered them precisely."
(The Holy Quran 19:94)

Keys to remember:

* People forget all the things you do for them. Especially all the little daily tasks. This is true for children who forget what their parents suffered for years for them. Spouses who forget what their spouse did day in and day out for years. Learners who forget what their teachers went through to teach them. However, we can find comfort in the fact that Allah never forgets anything. No matter how small or insignificant an act may seem, Allah knows and never forgets.

How this name effects my life:

_____
_____
_____
_____
_____
_____
_____

Al - Mubdi

المبدئ

Al-Mubdi,

The Starter, The Originator.

"And it is He who begins creation; then He repeats it, and that is [even] easier for Him. To Him belongs the highest attribute in the heavens and earth. And He is the Exalted in Might, the Wise."
(The Holy Quran 30:27)

"Is He [not best] who begins creation and then repeats it and who provides for you from the heaven and earth? Is there a deity with Allah ? Say, "Produce your proof, if you should be truthful."
(The Holy Quran 27:64)

Keys to remember:

* Non believers will refer to the big bang theory or evolution to explain creation. But if you ask them to go back to the very beginning when it all started, they will not be able to tell you with confidence what actually caused all the subsequent events to take place. Why suddenly after billions of years of emptiness would creation just start happening like that? It definitely needed at least something to spark it all off. That something is Allah's will and command. The beginning of everything in existence is from Him alone.

How this name effects my life:

_____

_____

_____

_____

_____

_____

Al - Mu'id

Al-Mu'id,

The Restorer, the Reinstater Who brings back all.

"To Him is your return all together. [It is] the promise of Allah which is] truth. Indeed, He begins the [process of] creation and then repeats it that He may reward those who have believed and done righteous deeds, in justice. But those who disbelieved will have a drink of scalding water and a painful punishment for what they used to deny."

(The Holy Quran 10:4)

Keys to remember:

★ Allah started the creation, He will end it all and then He will bring it all back again. It's very easy to be deceived in thinking that when this life ends that there is nothing after that. But Allah has left signs for us all around us that He in fact does bring life back again. Just observing how winter comes and takes away life from the trees, flowers... then how spring comes to restore it all again is evidence enough. This life is merely a bridge to our true and final one.

How this name effects my life:

_____
_____
_____
_____
_____
_____

Al - Muhyi

Al-Muhyi

The giver of life. He is the one Who creates life in all beings.

"How can you disbelieve in Allah when you were lifeless and He brought you to life; then He will cause you to die, then He will bring you [back] to life, and then to Him you will be returned."
(The Holy Quran 2:28)

"And He is the one who gave you life; then He causes you to die and then will [again] give you life. Indeed, mankind is ungrateful."
(The Holy Quran 22:66)

Keys to remember:

* Humans can be filled with pride all they wish, they can claim they have reached the peek of technology and science. But the fact is no matter what they do, they will stop helplessly in front of one simple fact. They can never ever, no matter how advanced they claim to be, give life. Allah alone has the ability to give life. Just pondering about this, should make us clearly feel how we are slaves to Allah. How everything is in His hands and that all we should truly be concerned with is pleasing Him not His creation.

How this name effects my life:

_____

_____

_____

_____

_____

_____

Al - Mumit

Al-Mumit

The Bringer of Death, The Destroyer.

"O you who have believed, do not be like those who disbelieved and said about their brothers when they traveled through the land or went out to fight, "If they had been with us, they would not have died or have been killed," so Allah makes that [misconception] a regret within their hearts. And it is Allah who gives life and causes death, and Allah is Seeing of what you do."

(The Holy Quran 3:156)

Keys to remember:

★ The only fact of life that we can all guarantee is that nothing lasts and all of us will leave. Just as Allah brings life, He brings death. Even though we need to work hard and do all what we can to build our life and strive for the best, we also need to remember this sad fact of life. At the end of the day no matter what we do we will leave. It's important to remember this so we can always keep our priorities in check and not be deceived by this temporary life.

How this name effects my life:

_____
_____
_____
_____
_____
_____

Al - Hai

Al - Hai

The Living. The Alive, the ever living. The One attributed with a life that is unlike our life and is not that of a combination of soul, flesh or blood.

"And rely upon the Ever-Living who does not die, and exalt [Allah] with His praise. And sufficient is He to be, with the sins of His servants, Acquainted"

(The Holy Quran 25,58)

"He is the Ever-Living; there is no deity except Him, so call upon Him, [being] sincere to Him in religion. [All] praise is [due] to Allah , Lord of the worlds."

(The Holy Quran 40,65)

Keys to remember:

★ We all go and none of us can depend 100% on anything in this life because everything goes and everything leaves. Allah is the only one that is always there and will always be there. Rely only on Allah and you will never lose.

How this name effects my life:

_____
_____
_____
_____
_____
_____

Al - Qayyum

القيوم

Al - Qayyum

The Self-Subsisting Sustainer of All, ,The Self existing, The One who remains and does not end.

"Allah - there is no deity except Him, the Ever-Living, the Sustainer of existence".

(The Holy Quran 3,2)

"And [all] faces will be humbled before the Ever-Living, the Sustainer of existence. And he will have failed who carries injustice."

(The Holy Quran 20,111)

Keys to remember:

* We can't live or function in anything without Allah's sustenance. Even one simple movement of an eye lid is from His sustenance and blessings. We rely upon Him in everything. Everything in existence relies upon Allah but Allah needs nothing from anyone. We should never rely on anyone but Allah because nothing will ever work without Allah's decree. We do need people's help in many things and it is important we do what is needed to prosper in life but it's also important that our hearts are connected with Allah and we are sure that everything is from Allah alone.

How this name effects my life:

_____
_____
_____
_____
_____
_____

Al - Waajid

الواجد

Al-Waajid

The Perceiver, The Finder, The Unfailing. The Rich who is never poor. Al-Wajd is Richness.

"Did He not find you an orphan and give [you] refuge? And He found you lost and guided [you], And He found you poor and made [you] self-sufficient."

(The Holy Quran 93,6-8)

Keys to remember:

★ What do you want in life? Health? Money? Faith? Love?.....Whatever you want in life, there is nothing too much or too big to ask for from Allah the most richest. The one who owns everything and the one whose riches never ever end. Ask from Him at all times and in anything and everything. More importantly have faith that He hears you and will answer you.

How this name effects my life:

_____
_____
_____
_____
_____
_____

Al - Maajid

The Glorious. The One who is with perfect power, high status, compassion, generosity, and kindness.

"And He is the Forgiving, the Affectionate, Honorable Owner of the Throne."

(The Holy Quran 85,14-15)

Keys to remember:

★ People are not perfect. If you find someone who is strong , they might not be compassionate. If they are compassionate , they might not be strong. If they have strength and compassion, they might not be wealthy. The only one who is perfect in all ways and has no defects in any way is Allah.

How this name effects my life:

_____
_____
_____
_____
_____
_____
_____

Al - Waahid

Al-Waahid,

The Unique, The One, The One without a partner.

"Say, "What thing is greatest in testimony?" Say, " Allah is witness between me and you. And this Qur'an was revealed to me that I may warn you thereby and whomever it reaches. Do you [truly] testify that with Allah there are other deities?" Say, "I will not testify [with you]." Say, "Indeed, He is but one God, and indeed, I am free of what you associate [with Him]."

(The Holy Quran 6,19)

Keys to remember:

★ When we think of the people in our lives, we usually think of them in terms of what makes them special and unique. It's easy to come up with 5 or even more qualities that makes that person special. But despite that, we can't say that there is no one else at all that is the same. Except when it comes to Allah, He is special and unique in more ways than we can ever count. And there is absolutely nothing that comes even close to Him.

How this name effects my life:

_____

_____

_____

_____

_____

_____

Al - Ahad

Al Ahad

The One, the All Inclusive, The Indivisible.

"Say, "He is Allah , [who is] One, Allah , the Eternal Refuge. He neither begets nor is born, Nor is there to Him any equivalent."
(The Holy Quran 112:1-4)

Keys to remember:

* One of the most beautiful chapters (surah) in the Quran that almost all Muslims love both adults and children is the chapter of Al-Ikhlas which means sincerity. The whole chapter is describing Allah and how He is the One that has no partners or anything like Him. While worshiping Allah, the most important thing we need to take care of is our sincerity and that our actions are done for Allah alone. It's important to always check our hearts and make sure our actions are only to please Him and not anyone else.

How this name effects my life:

_____

_____

_____

_____

_____

As - Samad

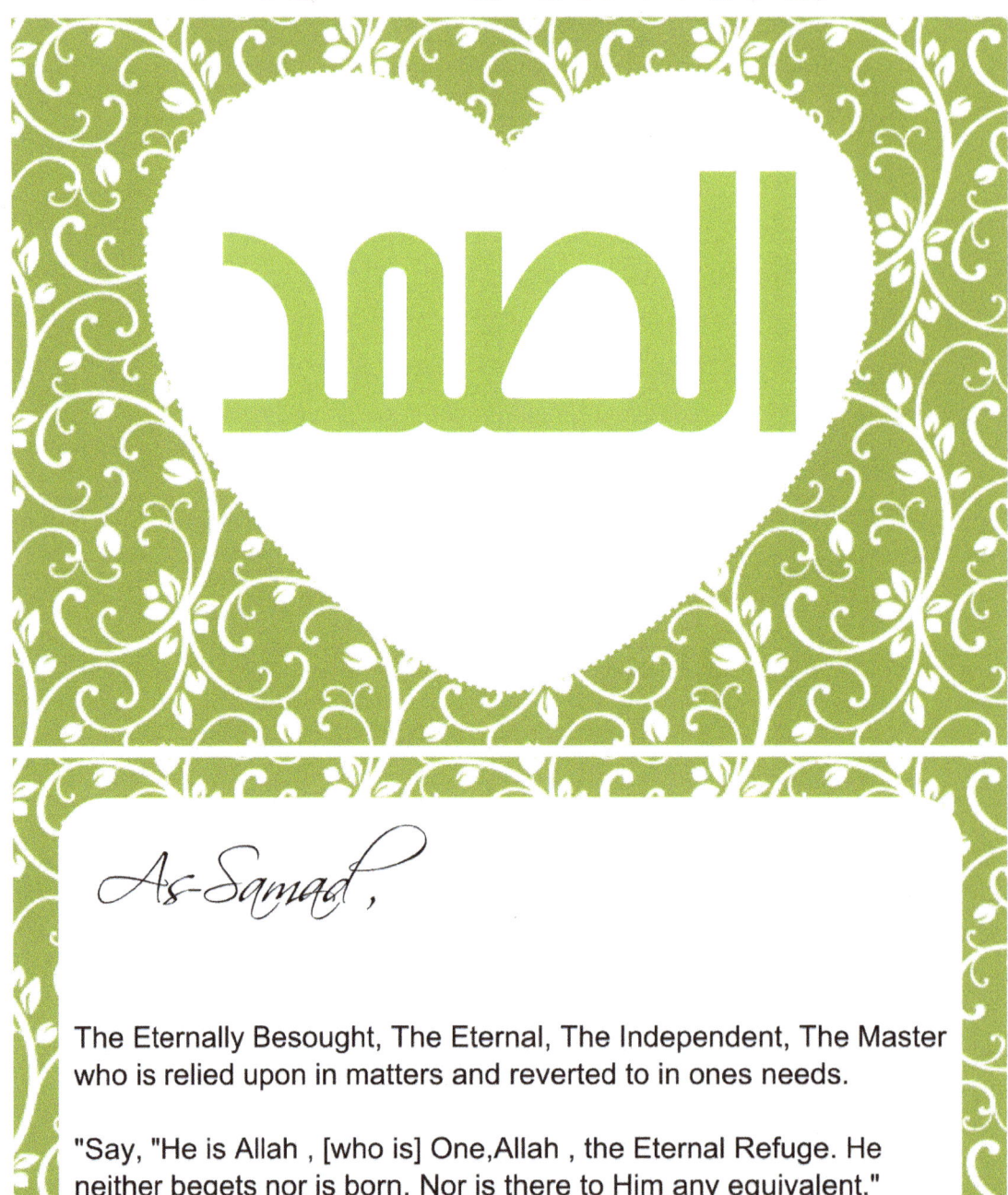

As-Samad,

The Eternally Besought, The Eternal, The Independent, The Master who is relied upon in matters and reverted to in ones needs.

"Say, "He is Allah , [who is] One,Allah , the Eternal Refuge. He neither begets nor is born, Nor is there to Him any equivalent."
(The Holy Quran 112,1-4)

Keys to remember:

* We all have that one person in our life or more if we're lucky who we know we can go to when things get tough. But again, every so often, we may go through something that even that person who we used to rely on can't be there for us whether it's by choice or by circumstance. The only one we can find limitless and eternal refuge in is Allah (swt). He is there for us at all times and in any place we are.

* If you want to find Allah next to you in times of need, make sure to go to Him always even at times of ease. He will hear you without you even needing to talk.

How this name effects my life:

_____
_____
_____
_____
_____

Al - Qaadir

Al - Qaadir,

The Omnipotent, The Able, The Capable, The One attributed with Power.

"Do they not see that Allah , who created the heavens and earth, is [the one] Able to create the likes of them? And He has appointed for them a term, about which there is no doubt. But the wrongdoers refuse [anything] except disbelief."

(The Holy Quran 17,99)

Keys to remember:

★ We all rely on different people in our lives for our diverse needs. Whether it be our emotional needs from friends and family or our livelihood needs from different people in our society. Naturally we don't mix these things, for example, we wouldn't go to a baker to fulfill our emotional needs. Each person has limited abilities, and hence their involvement in our life is bounded. There is only One who has boundless ability in every aspect we can even think of. Allah is the only one with the true power to give us what we want and need. No one in this world has power except from Him and by His will.

How this name effects my life:

_____

_____

_____

_____

_____

Al - Muqtadir

Al-Muqtadir,

The Powerful, The Dominant, The One with the perfect Power that nothing is withheld from Him.

"And present to them the example of the life of this world, [its being] like rain which We send down from the sky, and the vegetation of the earth mingles with it and [then] it becomes dry remnants, scattered by the winds. And Allah is ever, over all things, Perfect in Ability."

(The Holy Quran 18,45)

Keys to remember:

★ Who of us can claim to have perfect power over anything? Just a simple headache can make us feel how truly weak we are. No matter how clever we are or strong we are or beautiful...etc, these things all fade with time and there will always be someone who is better than us. We can never reach perfection in anything we do no matter how hard we try. It's important for us to realize this fact so we can be content with what Allah has given us and for pride not to enter our hearts and make us forget the true purpose we are here for. We are here to worship Allah alone and strive to please Him.

How this name effects my life:

_____
_____
_____
_____
_____
_____

Al - Muqaddim

Al-Muqaddim

The Expediter, The Promoter, The One who puts things in their right places. He makes ahead what He wills and delays what He wills.

"And if Allah was to hasten for the people the evil [they invoke] as He hastens for them the good, their term would have been ended for them. But We leave the ones who do not expect the meeting with Us, in their transgression, wandering blindly."

(The Holy Quran 10,11)

Keys to remember:

★ Allah chooses when things take place in our life. His choice is what is best for us and we can also be tested with His decree and His timing. As Muslims part of our faith is to submit to Allah's will, and that what He decrees is truly the best. It also should give us a sense of comfort that Allah is taking care of our affairs at all times and that everything that happens in the universe is with His will. The will of the most just , the most compassionate and the most perfect in all ways possible.

How this name effects my life:

_____
_____
_____
_____
_____
_____

Al - Mu'akhir

Al-Mu'akhir,

The Delayer, The One who puts things in their right places. He makes ahead what He wills and delays what He wills.

"Allah will forgive you of your sins and delay you for a specified term. Indeed, the time [set by] Allah, when it comes, will not be delayed, if you only knew.' "

(The Holy Quran 71,4)

"And if Allah were to impose blame on the people for their wrongdoing, He would not have left upon the earth any creature, but He defers them for a specified term. And when their term has come, they will not remain behind an hour, nor will they precede [it]."

(The Holy Quran 16,61)

Keys to remember:

★ So many times throughout our life we really want things and we ask Allah for it continuously. If we don't get what we want straight away we can mistakenly start thinking why didn't Allah give us what we want. It can be very hard for us to be at peace with not getting what we want. It takes faith to be truly content when Allah delays giving us something we want. To reach this content state we need to truly believe in this name of Allah. This names tells us that He puts everything in its right place at the right time. He knows what is best for us and we need to believe that.

How this name effects my life:

_____
_____
_____
_____
_____

Al - Awwal

Al - Awwal,

The First, The One whose Existence is without a beginning.

"He is the First and the Last, the Ascendant and the Intimate, and He is, of all things, Knowing."
(The Holy Quran 57,3)

"Leave Me with the one I created alone"
(The Holy Quran 74,11)

Keys to remember:

* For us as humans when we think of anything we think of it in terms of having a beginning and an end. It's impossible to imagine something with no beginning. For atheists who don't believe in Allah, it's easy to see how their disbelief is illogical. Everything in this universe has to have a beginning, but the only way that this can work is that there was something that created it all before everything came into existence. Allah is the first, the one that was there before anything and everything.

How this name effects my life:

_____

_____

_____

_____

_____

_____

_____

Al - Aakhir

Al - Aakhir,

The Last, The One whose Existence is without an end.

"He is the First and the Last, the Ascendant and the Intimate, and He is, of all things, Knowing."

(The Holy Quran 57,3)

Keys to remember:

* Everything has an end, all of us will cease to exist and everything we love will also leave one day. The only way that this world would make any sense, is that at the end there will be justice. The only way our existence could mean anything is that even though everything will end, there will be One left that will never ever end. Allah is the only One with no end, He is not limited by time in any way. Time is one of His creations, it doesn't effect Him in any way.

How this name effects my life:

_____

_____

_____

_____

_____

_____

_____

Az - Zaahir

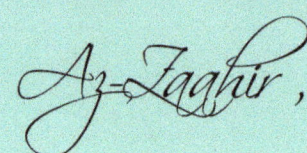

The Manifest, The One that nothing is above Him and nothing is underneath Him. He, The Exalted, His Existence is obvious by proofs and He is clear from the delusions of attributes of bodies.

"He is the First and the Last, the Manifest and the Intimate, and He is, of all things, Knowing."

(The Holy Quran 57,3)

Keys to remember:

★ The proof of Allah's existence is clear in everything around us. If someone is truly seeking the truth, they can easily see the proof. Allah would not punish us in the afterlife unless His existence and our obligation to have faith in Him was abundantly clear.

How this name effects my life:

_____
_____
_____
_____
_____
_____
_____

Al - Baatin

Al-Baatin,

The Hidden, The All Encompassing. The One that nothing is above Him and nothing is underneath Him, hence He exists without being contained in a place.

"He is the First and the Last, the Manifest and the Hidden, and He is, of all things, Knowing."

(The Holy Quran 57,3)

Keys to remember:

- ★ Allah is always there, at all times, no place or time bounds Him. We may not see Allah or hear Him but for sure He is there for us always.

How this name effects my life:

_____
_____
_____
_____
_____
_____
_____

Al - Muta'aalee

المتعالي

Al-Muta'aalee,

The Most Exalted, The High Exalted, The One who is clear from the attributes of the creation.

"[He is] Knower of the unseen and the witnessed, the Grand, the Exalted."

(The Holy Quran 13,9)

Keys to remember:

* It's important we always remember that Allah is above His creation and nothing in this world resembles Him. When we study His names and characteristics, it's important we don't think of them as we would think of human attributes. Allah is perfect in all ways, in ways we can't even imagine or comprehend. When we worship Allah, it's also important to know that we can never ever give Allah's rights due on us, what we can do is try our best to worship Allah in the way that pleases Him and then we ask for His mercy. No ones deeds will ever be the cause to enter paradise, we can only enter paradise with His mercy.

How this name effects my life:

_____
_____
_____
_____
_____

Al - Barr

Al - Barr,

The Source of All Goodness, The Righteous, The One who is kind to His creatures, who covered them with His sustenance and specified whoever He willed among them by His support, protection, and special mercy.

"Indeed, we used to supplicate Him before. Indeed, it is He who is the Source of All Goodness, the Merciful."
(The Holy Quran 52,28)

Keys to remember:

★ Allah is the source of all goodness. No evil comes from Allah. Anything seemingly bad that happens in this world has to have some benefit in it or it wouldn't take place. At many times the bad things that happen can serve as wake up calls for us so we are not deceived by the pleasures in this world and we realize this is only a temporary place that we will soon leave.

★ Allah is merciful with all His creatures , but He also gives special mercy to who He wills. Remembering Allah at all times and trying to please Him will bring this mercy in your life. It will bring you happiness like nothing else ever can.

How this name effects my life:

_____

_____

_____

_____

_____

At - Tawwaab

At - Tawwaab,

The Acceptor of Repentance, The Relenting, The One who grants repentance to whoever He willed among His creatures and accepts his repentance.

"And We did not send any messenger except to be obeyed by permission of Allah . And if, when they wronged themselves, they had come to you, [O Muhammad], and asked forgiveness of Allah and the Messenger had asked forgiveness for them, they would have found Allah Accepting of repentance and Merciful."

(The Holy Quran 4,64)

Keys to remember:

★ One of the biggest mistakes a Muslim can make is thinking that they have sinned so much that there is no way Allah would ever forgive them. It is the devil's trick to make a believer feel they have gone too far away from Allah that there is no way back. Allah calls Himself the Acceptor of repentance because this is something He continuously does. If we did not sin then this name would have no place in our lives, but in fact Allah's names are continuously reflected in our lives. No matter what we do we should always find comfort in the fact that Allah's door is always opened no matter what. All we need to do is to knock on that door and ask for forgiveness.

How this name effects my life:

_____

_____

_____

_____

_____

Al - Muntaqim

Al-Muntaqim

The Avenger. The One who victoriously prevails over His enemies and punishes them for their sins.

"Before, as guidance for the people. And He revealed the Qur'an. Indeed, those who disbelieve in the verses of Allah will have a severe punishment, and Allah is exalted in Might, the Avenger."
(The Holy Quran 3:4)

"So never think that Allah will fail in His promise to His messengers. Indeed, Allah is Exalted in Might and The Avenger."
(The Holy Quran 14:47)

Keys to remember:

★ It's very important when we reflect on the names of Allah, not to compare their characteristics to those of humans. This is also true when thinking of the name the Avenger. When we think of this name we may think of negative things, as we usually think of revenge as something negative. But in Allah's case, His names only describe perfection in all ways with nothing negative attached to them in any way. In this case, this name is related to Allah's justice. For it is only just that for the people who committed wrong, Allah takes revenge on them. It is part of Allah's mercy, justice and wisdom that not everyone will be treated the same. But in fact they will be rewarded or punished according to their deeds.

How this name effects my life:

_____

_____

_____

Al - 'Afuww

Al-'Afuww,

The Pardoner, The Forgiver, The One with wide forgiveness.

"And [recall] when We said, "Enter this city and eat from it wherever you will in [ease and] abundance, and enter the gate bowing humbly and say, 'Relieve us of our burdens.' We will [then] forgive your sins for you, and We will increase the doers of good [in goodness and reward]."

(The Holy Quran 2,58)

Keys to remember:

★ Even though this name seems to have the same meaning as the name (Al-Ghafour), however there is a distinct difference between them. Looking at the of roots of the words in the Arabic language, you will find that (Al -'Afuww) means forgiveness with all traces and marks completely removed. Meaning that Allah will not only forgive the sins but they will be completely removed from the record of deeds. On the day of Judgment no one will be aware of them, even the person who committed them won't remember committing them.

How this name effects my life:

_____

_____

_____

_____

_____

_____

Ar - Ra'oof

Ar-Ra'oof,

The Most Kind, The Compassionate, The One with extreme Mercy. The Mercy of Allah is His will to endow upon whoever He willed among His creatures.

"The Day every soul will find what it has done of good present [before it] and what it has done of evil, it will wish that between itself and that [evil] was a great distance. And Allah warns you of Himself, and Allah is Kind to [His] servants."

(The Holy Quran 3,30)

"And [there is a share for] those who came after them, saying, "Our Lord, forgive us and our brothers who preceded us in faith and put not in our hearts [any] resentment toward those who have believed. Our Lord, indeed You are Kind and Merciful."

(The Holy Quran 59,10)

Keys to remember:

★ Extreme mercy, extreme compassion, extreme kindness all in one. If any of us think of the qualities we would love to have in the people around us , these three qualities would probably top the list. People can have some of these qualities some of the time, but to have all of them to the extreme all the time is truly an impossibility. How can anyone ever lose if they have the one with all of these qualities on their side. Life may be very difficult but it's only a temporary stage. Never let the difficulties of this life make you forget that Allah is always there for you with these amazing qualities that only He has.

How this name effects my life:

_____

_____

_____

_____

_____

Maalik - ul - Mulk

مالك الملك

Maalik-ul-Mulk

The Owner of Sovereignty, The Eternal Owner of Sovereignty, The One who controls the Dominion and gives dominion to whoever He willed.

"Say, "O Allah , Owner of Sovereignty, You give sovereignty to whom You will and You take sovereignty away from whom You will. You honor whom You will and You humble whom You will. In Your hand is [all] good. Indeed, You are over all things competent."
(The Holy Quran 3,26)

Keys to remember:

- People may falsely call themselves kings in this world, but the truth is no one can ever truly be king except Allah. No one can ever own the land and everything in it except Allah.

- If a slave tries his best to get closer to his king this is something to be expected and totally natural. But what about the king of all of creation coming down to earth in the last third of the night and calling upon us so He can answer our prayers, give us what we want and forgive our sins. Truly, perfection in all ways only belongs to Allah.

How this name effects my life:

_____
_____
_____
_____
_____

Dhul - Jalaali Wal - Ikraam

Dhul-Jalaali Wal-Ikraam

Majestic and Benevolent, The Lord of Majesty and Bounty, The One who deserves to be Exalted and not denied.

"And there will remain the Face of your Lord, Owner of Majesty and Honor"
(The Holy Quran 55,27)

"Blessed is the name of your Lord, Owner of Majesty and Honor."
(The Holy Quran 55,78)

Keys to remember:

★ People can become very proud of themselves and feel they deserve to be treated with up most respect and honour. Even though most of the time they are proud of things that they did not contribute at all in obtaining such as beauty, money and lineage. Not only are they proud but even the people around them treat them as if they have some kind of privilege over others. All the while forgetting that these are merely blessings from Allah and they bare no weight in the actual true value of a person. There is only one who is worthy of ultimate majesty and honour and that is Allah (swt).

How this name effects my life:

_____
_____
_____
_____

Al - Muqsit

Al-Muqsit

The Just, The Lord of Majesty and Bounty, The One who deserves to be Exalted and not denied.

"Allah witnesses that there is no deity except Him, and [so do] the angels and those of knowledge - [that He is] maintaining [creation] in justice. There is no deity except Him, the Exalted in Might, the Wise."

(The Holy Quran 3,18)

Keys to remember:

★ In a world full of daily injustices, how do we find peace? We find peace by knowing that Allah in fact is just and everyone will get what they deserve whether good or bad. We need to realize that as humans our understanding and perception is very limited. We only see our small circle and what we want, we don't see the bigger picture and how things are intertwined. Even if we see a whole country being subjected to severe injustice for 100 years, what is 100 years in the scale of the human existence (approx 200,000 years) and what is the existence of humanity compared to the existence of the universe (approx 15 billion years). Our lives are limited and so is our view of the world, we need to trust in our creator that only He knows what is best and how and when things should take place.

How this name effects my life:

_____

_____

_____

_____

Al - Jaami'

Al-Jaami'

The Gatherer, The One who gathers the creatures on a day that there is no doubt about, that is the Day of Judgment.

"Our Lord, surely You will gather the people for a Day about which there is no doubt. Indeed, Allah does not fail in His promise.""
(The Holy Quran 3,9)

Keys to remember:

★ This life separates people even the closest of families and friends. Even though this is very painful for us, however, this life will end either way and if we are among the believers Allah will gather us all together again in paradise.

★ Don't forget to continuously ask Allah the only one who can gather us, to gather you with your loved ones in the next life.

How this name effects my life:

_____
_____
_____
_____
_____
_____
_____

Al - Ghaniyy

Al-Ghaniyy

The Self-Sufficient, The One who does not need the creation.

"Kind speech and forgiveness are better than charity followed by injury. And Allah is Free of need and Forbearing."
　　　　　　　　　　　　　　　(The Holy Quran 2,263)

"In it are clear signs [such as] the standing place of Abraham. And whoever enters it shall be safe. And [due] to Allah from the people is a pilgrimage to the House - for whoever is able to find thereto a way. But whoever disbelieves - then indeed, Allah is free from need of the worlds."　　　　　　　　　　(The Holy Quran 3,97)

Keys to remember:

- Allah doesn't benefit anything from our worship or our praise to Him. We are the ones who benefit from it, when we worship Him it is us who benefit. It's like when we are ill and we follow the doctor's advice, we are the ones who will benefit from the advice. The doctor will not benefit anything, neither will he lose anything if we choose not to listen.
- Any good acts or worship you do is for your benefit and it's not something to be proud of in front of Allah or people. It's a blessing we should thank Allah for.

How this name effects my life:

_____

_____

_____

_____

_____

_____

_____

Al - Mughnee

Al-Mughnee,

The Enricher, The One who satisfies the necessities of the creatures.

"O' you who have believed, indeed the polytheists are unclean, so let them not approach al-Masjid al-Haram after this, their [final] year. And if you fear privation, Allah will enrich you from His bounty if He wills. Indeed, Allah is Knowing and Wise."

(The Holy Quran 9,28)

Keys to remember:

★ Allah provides sustenance for everything in existence from the smallest to the biggest. He is the one and only one who can give you everything you have ever wanted.

★ Make sure to ask Allah for everything you want and need. While asking from Allah it's important to take practical steps to attain what you want. When you do get what you want it's important you know that at the end of the day everything comes from Allah.

How this name effects my life:

_____
_____
_____
_____
_____
_____
_____

Al - Maani'

Al-Maani',

The Preventer of Harm. The Preventer, The Withholder, The Shielder, The Defender.

To obtain Allah's protection throughout the day and night, make sure to recite the daily authentic azkar narrated by the prophet Mohamed (peace be upon him). There are azkar to be said at morning and night and others for specific acts such as entering the bathroom or leaving the house or before sleeping and so on.

Keys to remember:

- Make sure to seek Allah's protection at all times, ultimately He is the only one who controls your life and can save you from harm. You also need to make sure that this is done according to Quran and authentic sunnah. Unfortunately, there are many acts that some Muslims do in an attempt to protect themselves from harm, however they do not get the protection they seek and worse than that at many times they unknowingly commit shirk. Some of these things is wearing amulets, going to fortune tellers, doing magic, asking protection from the dead,....etc.

How this name effects my life:

_____
_____
_____
_____
_____

Ad - Daar

Ad - Daar,

The Distresser, The One who makes harm reach to whoever He wills and benefit to whoever He wills.

"Young man, (the Prophet said to Abdullah ibn al-Abbas) hear some words of advice: Be mindful of God and God will protect you. Be mindful of God and you will find Him before you. If you ask, ask of God; if you seek help, seek help of God. Know that if all the people were to gather together to give you the benefit of anything, it would be something that God had already prescribed for you, and that if they gathered together to harm you with anything, this would only be as God had already ordained." Hadith of At-Tirmidhi.

Keys to remember:

★ He is the only one who controls this universe and everything that happens in it. Everything happens with His decree. However, it's also important to note that any harm that happens to us is either a punishment for our own sins or it's a test from Allah to test our faith and purify us. At the end anything that happens to us is for our good even if we can't understand it at the time.

How this name effects my life:

_____

_____

_____

_____

_____

_____

_____

An - naafi'

النافع

An-Naafi'

The Propitious, The Benefactor. The One who benefits whoever He wills.

"And He gave you from all you asked of Him. And if you should count the favor of Allah, you could not enumerate them. Indeed, mankind is [generally] most unjust and ungrateful."

(The Holy Quran 14,34)

Keys to remember:

★ Allah is the source of all benefit, no one can benefit us in any way unless Allah allows it. We should always ask from Allah and rely on Him alone.

★ We should always remember to ask Allah for the best in this world and for the best in the next.

How this name effects my life:

_____
_____
_____
_____
_____
_____
_____

An - Noor

النور

An-Noor,

The Light. His light lightens up the whole world, whether it be the heavens and earth or the believers' hearts.

"Allah is the Light of the heavens and the earth. The example of His light is like a niche within which is a lamp, the lamp is within glass, the glass as if it were a pearly [white] star lit from [the oil of] a blessed olive tree, neither of the east nor of the west, whose oil would almost glow even if untouched by fire. Light upon light. Allah guides to His light whom He wills. And Allah presents examples for the people, and Allah is Knowing of all things."

(The Holy Quran 24,35)

Keys to remember:

★ They aim to extinguish God's light with their utterances but God has willed to spread His light in all its fullness, however hateful this may be to all who deny the truth.
The Holy Quran (6:18)

★ A wonderful supplication of the prophet (peace be upon him) that we should also say 'O Allah, place within my heart light, and upon my tongue light, and within my ears light, and within my eyes light, and place behind me light and in front of me light and above me light and beneath me light. O Allah, bestow upon me light.'
(mentioned in Bukhari and Muslim)

How this name effects my life:

_____
_____
_____
_____
_____
_____

Al - Haadee

الهادي

Al - Haadee,

The Guide, The Propitious, The One who guides whoever he wishes and sends astray whoever he wishes.

"And thus have We made for every prophet an enemy from among the criminals. But sufficient is your Lord as a guide and a helper."
(The Holy Quran 25,31)

Keys to remember:

* Allah knows what is in the hearts, He knows who is worthy of guidance and who isn't. We may meet people in our life that we wish so badly that they would be guided but no matter what we do they don't change. Allah knows best and we need to know that guidance comes from Him alone.

* A very good prayer to say to help keep us on the path of guidance from the Quran (3:8) is:

"ربنا لا تزغ قلوبنا بعد إذ هديتنا وهب لنا من لدنك رحمة إنك أنت الوهاب".

[Who say], "Our Lord, let not our hearts deviate after You have guided us and grant us from Yourself mercy. Indeed, You are the Bestower.

How this name effects my life:

_____
_____
_____
_____

Al - Badee'

Al-Badee'

The Originator. The One who creates with ultimate beauty.

"Originator of the heavens and the earth. When He decrees a matter, He only says to it, "Be," and it is."
(The Holy Quran 2,117)

He creates with beauty and originality that is beyond our capacity. Anything a human makes or invents will always mimic something that is already in nature. Allah is the only one who can create from scratch.

Keys to remember:

★ One of the neglected kinds of worship is "tafakor" which is reflecting on Allah's creation. It's a form of worship because when you truly reflect on the creation around you and how beautiful and perfect it is and how no one else can ever create anything like it your faith in Allah will increase. The more your faith increases from the things you can see in front of you, the easier it is to also believe in the unseen as it is all from the same source. Try and set a time each day or even each week where you can just sit and reflect on the beauty of creation around you. You can reflect on the creation of your own body, the skies, the plants, the animals,...there are countless examples around you that manifest clearly the beauty of Allah's creation.

How this name effects my life:

_____

_____

_____

_____

Al - Baaqee

Al-Baaqee,

The Everlasting. The Ever Enduring and Immutable.

"And there will remain the Face of your Lord, Owner of Majesty and Honor."

(The Holy Quran 55,27)

Allah is eternal; He is without beginning and without end. Everything in the universe will perish except Him.

Keys to remember:

★ It's so comforting and relieving to know that Allah is always there for you. If the whole world desserts you and turns their back you, if you have Allah on your side then it doesn't matter. If you have Allah in your life, you have everything you need because He will never leave you and He will always give you the best.

How this name effects my life:

_____

_____

_____

_____

_____

_____

_____

Al - Waarith

The Heir, The Ultimate Inheritor of all.

"And indeed, it is We who give life and cause death, and We are the Inheritor."

(The Holy Quran 15,23)

"And how many a city have We destroyed that was insolent in its [way of] living, and those are their dwellings which have not been inhabited after them except briefly. And it is We who were the inheritors."

(The Holy Quran 28,58)

Keys to remember:

* Studying history and what happened to past nations is very important to understand the true value of life and what our priorities should be. Reflecting back in history we can see that it didn't matter how advance a nation was or how much wealth they accumulated, at the end of the day every nation that was against following Allah's commands was destroyed. Our lives are short no matter how long we live, we get one chance to worship Allah so it's important we don't waste it.

How this name effects my life:

_____
_____
_____
_____
_____
_____

Ar - Rasheed

Ar-Rasheed,

The Guide to the Right Path.

"Guide us to the straight path"
(The Holy Quran 1,6)

The most important thing in this life is that we are guided to the right path. That is why we invoke Allah asking for his guidance at least 17 times a day through our prayers and the recitation of surah Al-Fatiha.

Keys to remember:

★ We may think we are strong in our faith and that we have no problem staying on the straight path. However, we never know how our hearts could change and we can suddenly find ourselves completely off the path. It's important to always check on ourselves and try to increase our faith and level of good deeds. Ultimately the most important thing is to ask Allah to keep us stead fast on the right path.

How this name effects my life:

_____

_____

_____

_____

_____

_____

_____

As - Saboor

As-Saboor,

The Patient, The Timeless.

Allah is patient with us, because of his mercy He does not punish us straight away. He gives us many chances to repent and sends us many signs. For example when we do a good deed it is recorded by the angels straight away, however if we commit a bad deed the angels do not record the deed until 6 hours later to give us a chance to repent. Allah is also the source of patience, for when we meet with calamities we turn to Him to give us the necessary patience to help us bear anything we go through.

Keys to remember:

★ People can be patient, they can put up with a lot but they have their limits. If they are treated badly by someone they may not retaliate, they might even respond in a good way rather than a bad way but how many times can they do that? We can truly realize how amazing and great Allah is while just reflecting on this one quality, patience. Many people don't worship Allah at all, sin day and night, do acts that invoke His anger but Allah doesn't punish straight away. He gives us chance after chance after chance to fix ourselves. Not only does He not punish us while we deserve it but He continues to give us life, and provide us with all what we need, food, drink, health, shelter...etc. His patience truly has no parallel.

How this name effects my life:

_____

_____

_____

_____

_____

Halah Azim
Understand & Love your creator - Learn the 99 names of Allah

© 2014, Halah Azim
www.theheartsoflight.com

About the author: Halah Azim is a British/Egyptian Muslim living in Australia. She has a B.A in computer engineering from Cairo and she also completed a 2 year diploma in Islamic studies from Cairo. Currently she is working on her B.A in extensive Islamic studies from the Islamic Online University.

To get more unique Islamic products for the whole family visit: www.theheartsoflight.com and make sure to join us on facebook, www.facebook.com/TheHeartsOfLight

ALL RIGHTS RESERVED. This book contains material protected under International and Federal Copyright Laws and Treaties. Any unauthorized reprint or use of this material is prohibited. No part of this book may be reproduced or

www.ingramcontent.com/pod-product-compliance
Lightning Source LLC
Chambersburg PA
CBHW061811290426
44110CB00026B/2849